AF478816

Hex codes, or hexadecimal codes, are a way to represent colors in digital devices and web design. Each hex code refers to a very specific color. A hex color is expressed as a six-digit combination of numbers and letters, preceded by a pound sign or hashtag, defined by its mix of red, green, and blue (RGB). The first two letters or numbers refer to red, the next two refer to green, and the last two refer to blue.

The color values are defined as values between 00 and FF. Hex codes are a universal way to describe colors. This book is specifically about shades of white.

c is for china ivory

#FCFFE7

D is for double pearl lusta

D

#FCF4D0

d is for dutch white

d

#EFDFBB

e is for eggshell

#F0EAD6

j is for jasmine white

#F6F2E7

N is for natural white

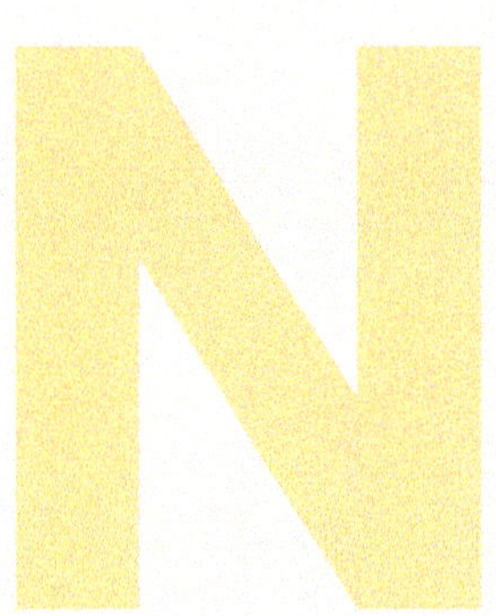

#FBEDE5

n is for navajo white

#FFDEAD

q is for quietlywhisper

t is for travertine

#FFFDE8

U is for ultra white
U
#9F2EC

u is forumber style

U

#ECEöDA

X is for x-50 crystal white

#F4F3EB

x is for x-73 eggshell white

#EBE4D2

y is for yucca white

#EDEBD4

Z is for zinc white

Z

#E1D8D0

z is for zurich white

z

#E7E2DA